What readers are saying about

"The Proper Production (or Project) Meeting"

"Productive meetings are crucial to achieve the desired results in any project or manufacturing plant. Jim Thompson summarizes his decades of experience in our industry with an easy to read and good guidance book that provides a clear meeting methodology and tips to improve leadership, team work and people engagement. I recommend it for anyone that has to manage meetings in our industry."

Francisco Carilla
Group Industrial Project Director
SAICA
Zaragoza, Spain

"My actionable item from reading this book is to strongly recommend it! And if your meetings are like "Frank's" this is a great blueprint to initiate change and start anew. The production meeting as envisioned by Jim will be the most important activity you participate in toward being successful and, of course, spinning the invoice printer."

Gary W. Nyman
SME Innovative Solutions
International Paper-Technology
Chapin, South Carolina

a

"Functional teams drawn from across the business are universally recognized by manufacturers as essential for success, but being teams, effectiveness varies wildly. Attending a meeting for even a few minutes shows this, and of all meetings, the routine production meeting is the most illustrative of the organization. Effective team work requires a leader willing to establish rules, set expectations and maintain discipline. In 'The Proper Production (or Project) Meeting' Jim Thompson again teaches with clarity how to transform the production meeting, and the team, from mediocrity to excellence. The task is simple to describe, but difficult to execute, as it may force tough, therefore unpopular, actions. The book is directed to the Operations (or Project) Manager, but it is also an excellent guide for any team member. There is considerable satisfaction leading effective teams, especially as the skills can be learned, as shown here by Jim."

Dene H. Taylor, Ph.D.
President
SPF—Inc.
New Hope, Pennsylvania

b

"This quick read is guaranteed to give you at least one good idea that will improve your leadership and communication effectiveness. Praise in public; admonish in private; love it!"

Gene Canavan
US Army (ret.)
International Paper (ret.)
Prattville, Alabama

"Jim has again taken on a subject with rigor and crushing logic. His decades of experience and retrospect allow him to opine with authority, and he has! This is a must read for young industry professionals and all others who are interested in doing these jobs well."

Ed Graf
Consultant and Inventor
Washington Island, Wisconsin

"I find Jim's ideas and tips to be on-point here. I've used similar formats and structure for my production meetings over time and have experienced some of the wins and trip-ups illustrated here. I can certainly recommend this easy, quick read book for helping achieve excellence. I'm already using some of his points to improve my own production meeting."

Joe Hasson
Plant Manager
EG Industries
Ormond Beach, Florida

"Jim Thompson adroitly addresses the bane of inefficient and ineffective meetings and outlines a sensible and feasible corrective action plan. Good work, Jim. Here's to better meetings all!"

D. Lloyd Monroe IV
Of Counsel, Coppins & Monroe, P.A.
Tallahassee, Florida
Co-founder/Director, Porch de Salomon
Panajachel, Guatemala

The Proper Production (or Project) Meeting

Essentials for daily accountability and goal achievement

By

Jim Thompson

First Printing, March 2018

ISBN 978-0-9998248-1-8

This book is dedicated to

the wonderful people

who step up and make business move forward, either

daily in a production meeting or by leading a special

project.

You make free enterprise hum.

Table of Contents

Prelude

Having observed and conducted project, then production meetings for nearly half a century, I have some constructive thoughts to offer on the subject. These apply to manufacturing, and in some cases warehousing, operations across all industries. There is only one distinction to be made—are we talking about a seven-day, 24-hour operation or a five-day operation? We will discuss both of these variants as we progress, for they do have some minor differences.

The principles promulgated in this book can also be used to manage large one-off projects, for a large project has all the characteristics of production with the exception that it has a definite end date when the objective of the project is achieved.

In all cases, a leader must gather, encourage, challenge, correct and praise a disparate group of managers and transient visitors (staff personnel, consultants, suppliers) towards a common goal. These group members will be of various experience levels, maturity (career as well as general life) and possess their own agenda and objectives. It is the leader's job to set the tone, set the pace, set the expectations, and achieve the results. This is a tall order and an assignment not to be taken lightly.

Over the years I have seen highly competent production meeting leaders, completely incompetent production meeting leaders, and everything in between. I will attempt to lead you, the reader, in a way that you can at least start in the upper quartile of competence and then inspire you to become one of the best.

I must warn those of you who recognize, upon reading this book, that you who have not been in at least the upper half performance level in your leadership skills are going to have a difficult time. Why? Your team already knows your slack tolerances and low standards. Improving these will cause them to ask, "Why the change?" My recommendation is that you come clean and tell your team you have "seen the light" or had an epiphany. However you do it, acknowledge that it is a new day and things are going to be done differently from now on. You cannot ease into this change in modus operandi—once you decide to do it, it must be quick, decisive and with no looking back. Yet, it must be done with preparation and within this book I will help you prepare.

Finally, let me say that my objective in writing this book is to help you make your life easier, achieve your production or project goals, and, most importantly, allow you to sleep at night.

Peace be with you.

Chapter 1—Frank's dilemma

Frank, the production manager at Interesting Products, LLC, admitted that he had completely lost control of his production meeting. Attendance was sporadic; sometimes all departments were present, other days, some were absent with no explanations. Tardiness was rampant as was leaving early. Those present were often on their phones or two-way radios. When questioned during the meeting, the most common answer from attendees was, "I'll have to get back to you on that." Frank's boss often stuck her head in the door in the middle of the meeting and asked a question, either directed at Frank or one of his team members. Most importantly, attendees often left with no clear understanding of what they were to accomplish before the group regathered at the next appointed time (what I call the "Coming Period" throughout this book).

Frank was undoubtedly a poor leader.

Poor leaders are not born that way, someone failed to train them and promoted them before they were ready (it happened to me when I was young—don't try to hide it or be embarrassed by it—fix it!).

Let's make a list of the things that are wrong with Frank's production meeting:

1. Attendance was presumed to be optional.
2. Accountability, as evidenced by departments absent, was not considered important,

3. Respect for the meeting and the leader was non-existent, as evidenced by
   a. Tardiness
   b. Leaving early
   c. Talking on or texting via phone
   d. Two-way radio usage
   e. Not being prepared ("I'll have to get back to you on that")
   f. Frank's boss has no respect for Frank, the meeting, or both
4. Attendees leaving the meeting with no clear assignments or objectives.
5. Standards are so low that poor performers face no consequences and great performers receive no recognition.

Let's look at the background cost challenges in this facility.

We'll start with the cost of the meeting itself. Ten people are supposed to attend this meeting and have an average salary of $95,000 per year. With a burden of 33%, each one of these individuals is costing the company $126,350 per year or $60.75/hour. So, just convening this meeting for an hour cost $607.45 or slightly more than $10.00/minute.

Of course, for this bunch this is unimpressive, for they are averaging an hour a day of downtime, which is a lost contribution cost of $10,000.[1] Perhaps we should take that out of their pay, maybe we'll get their attention then, eh?

---

[1] I have seen this number be as high as $50,000/hour, but in that case the cost of the people sitting around the table is much higher, so I am attempting to keep costs in proportion here.

They are also running 5% returns and allowances (the cost of defective products or deliveries) and their facility is operating at a 92% efficiency rate in an industry that benchmarks at 95%.

Further, their poor product quality and delivery fulfillment record is causing the sales department to pull its hair out trying to maintain enough credit-qualified customers to keep the facility's production schedule full, even at the poor efficiency level they are experiencing.

This, in turn, has pushed the collection metric, DSO (Day's Sales Outstanding), to 50 from an industry average of 32, stressing the company's revolving credit line and jeopardizing its overall credit rating. In a climate of rising interest rates, the interest premium lenders are demanding for this poor performance leaves the future of the company in doubt—debt service costs are ballooning.

As if things could not get any worse, Frank has a couple of jewels on his team, professionals that would be essential to any turnaround. He's heard rumors that they are thinking about leaving.

This entire mess can be laid at the feet of one phenomenon: Frank's poor production meeting.

Further, Frank is not sleeping well (see the Prelude), and it is not just because of the night and weekend (his is a 24/7 operation) calls he is receiving.

We'll spend the rest of our time together fixing this.

Chapter 2—The Objective and Positioning of the Production (or Project) Meeting

What is the function and objective of the daily production meeting?

The Daily Production Meeting exists to set a short term strategic plan (that is, until its members meet again—the end of the "Coming Period") with the sole objective of equipping the members to tactically execute, with personal accountability, the Coming Period with the objective of beating the production facility's best production record up to this point in time.

To do this, the meeting will be used to report on what has happened since the last meeting, review any weaknesses in the path of setting a new production record in the Coming Period, and to offer support and encouragement to those individuals or departments whose contributory efforts towards this end may be in jeopardy.

Finally, public praise will be lavished on those whose performance exceeds expectations.

Daily, everything, and I mean everything, must revolve around the production meeting. If you want to have a physical image of the production meeting, imagine a forest full of vines. The primates, ahem, the meeting attendees, progress through the forest swinging from vine to vine. In a production setting, the trees and vines arc around in a circle, starting over every seventh tree (think of a week—seven days) and in a project, the trees and vines are arranged linearly, ending at a Pot of Gold. The gatherings of the primates in the trees represents the meeting and the swinging from vine to vine represents the time between meetings.

Production meetings happen whether production is operating or not (in a 24/7 operation; five-day operations usually get the weekends off except in cases of extremis). Seven-day operations even have meetings on the holidays.

The production meeting is the lifeblood of the organization. It is the centering point where everyone gathers, reports on the past period, shares plans for the Coming Period and/or receives direction for the Coming Period. Operated properly, it is vital to the health of the organization for it is the only time all managing departments are together and all can hear the plans, concerns and praises earned by the production unit as a whole. There is no more important hour in the day for any operating facility or project.

Most organizations as I have described here nominally understand the necessity of a production meeting or project meeting. I am a witness to this, for I have been in production facilities all over North America, some in Europe and some in South America—every one of them has had a daily production meeting.

Yet while most understand the *necessity*, if to no further depth than to know their peers have such a meeting, so they should, too—few understand the *importance*. Fewer still understand how to wring every last bit of *value* out of such a meeting.

Some leaders, such as Frank, think the meetings should be overly friendly. Frank mistakenly thinks a light-hearted atmosphere will engender comradery. That may be so, but what Frank is missing is that the meeting is for communication purposes, accountability recognition and to encourage and inspire people to do better in the Coming Period than in the just completed Period. It is not a party.

Do you know that every sports team has production meetings? Baseball, football, basketball and other sports have a production meeting before each game. Some sports, such as football and basketball, have a production meeting at half time. Many a game outcome, in fact almost all game outcomes, are the result of good or poor leadership in these production meetings.

While Frank thinks production meetings should be light-hearted, this is not universally the case and it is quite obvious such a stance is not working for Frank. A production meeting leader must know when to be light-hearted, when to be stern and when to be tough, just like a sports coach. Not to worry, these skills can be acquired.

A bit about being tough. Berating people is not appropriate. In all cases, everyone should be treated with respect. I witnessed a situation one time at a meeting of the production staff (although it was not at our regular time, but 8:00 in the evening when our monthly results were due at headquarters) where our leader threw a chair in the direction of the facility accountant. It was closing day for the previous month and, despite our three week lookahead predicting a profit, we had once again come up short for the month just past. This inspired no one to do anything except consider leaving and I think if the accountant had been so inclined, he could have pressed assault charges—he had plenty of witnesses, albeit they would have been reluctant witnesses. I can tell you for a fact, for some weeks to come, the accountant had one whole side of the conference room table to himself!

I have also witnessed particularly grim production meetings, in another facility, where our inhouse public relations official thought he would lighten the mood by telling a joke. Our mood was not lightened, in fact, those of us tasked with making a buck on a daily basis were resentful of his position and his attitude. A hint for all: unless you are a professional comedian (and then why are you here?) telling jokes usually doesn't work and these days can engender more ill will than good—it seems as though you can't tell a joke without offending someone these days.

Pleasant or stern, all business but always respectful.

Chapter 3—Set the Stage like you are setting the Stage

As you go about your transformation, hopefully your facility has enough space that you can requisition a new (to your production team) room for your new and enlightened production meeting. It doesn't have to be a fancy room, in fact I would not recommend you start with a fancy room. (Project teams, especially construction project teams, often meet in a trailer). It does not have to have windows. If it does, close the blinds. We are here for business.

The room should be clean to the standards you want for your entire facility and it must be maintained to this level of cleanliness at all times. I have seen production meeting rooms that look like they were evacuated due to a fire alarm—production samples all over the floor, broken pieces of equipment dragged in for "show and tell" dripping oil and so forth and so on. The room should be clean when people enter it and cleaner when they leave—every time.

This room should not be an extension of anyone's office. It should stand alone on its own merits as the hallowed and sacred place the production team determines the fate of the company on a day-to-day basis (OK, maybe that is overly dramatic, but perhaps you needed such a picture to get the point for this is exactly what it is).

Folding tables will do to start as well as cheap plastic chairs. Let the production team earn better furniture as results improve. At least one wall should have dry-erasable (or chalk) boards. A large screen television connected to a computer are optional elements at the start but will become essential as the meeting evolves.

The room should be well lit, so everyone can see their papers and write in comfort.

In the corner near the writing surface, which should be at the end of the room opposite where the leader sits (so all can see any illustrations on the writing surfaces) there should be a little credenza or cabinet with paper pads, pencils, dry erase pens, and so forth that may be needed during the course of the meeting. We don't want a break in the action for anyone to go acquire these materials—remember, their absence is costing us at least $10/minute for every minute the group must wait on something. This is not counting the cost of the time to get everyone back on subject after a break in the action. Someone (not necessarily a member of the group) should be assigned and held accountable for keeping the supplies regularly restocked.

Over the writing surface should be a large and accurate clock.

The room should not be a path to anywhere else—no one's shortcut. It should have one door only for both entrance and egress. It should be within hearing distance of any fire alarm or emergency alarm typical on the premises. It must not have a land line telephone. It should not be within hearing distance of any production machine break alarm. During the meeting, the only reason anyone will leave, other than a bona fide case of diarrhea, is because a personnel safety alarm has been activated. Treat the occupants and subjects discussed in this room as you would a sequestered jury.

Outside the door to this room, on a stand or a chair, we'll start with an adequately sized corrugated box with its top neatly removed. In this box, all attendees will place their cell phones, personal and company, as well as any two-way radios or other communications devices. Later, when they are being rewarded with upgraded chairs and a nice conference table, a local cabinet maker can build a custom set of cubbies to hold the phones and radios. This will be hung on the wall outside the room.

The leader's chair shall be no different than anyone else's (and by the way, if you still have personalized parking places in your parking lot, this is as good a time as any to get rid of these). And—some of you will be surprised at this statement—the leader's chair shall be the same height as all the other chairs in the room.

The chalkboard or white board shall be clean when everyone arrives and clean when everyone leaves. If material on the writing surfaces is deemed important enough to be preserved as determined by the leader, after the meeting is over and the room evacuated, a designee can enter and snap photos of the material to disseminate as the leader directs. In this case, the "photographer" shall clean the boards.

Optional, but not necessary, is a neatly manufactured sign over the writing surfaces that says "Spinnin' the invoice printer." On the wall over the Leader is a sign that says "Legal, Moral and Ethical" and on one of the side walls (opposite the door if the door is in a side wall) is a sign reading "Lean, Orderly and Clean."

Outside the room, on the door, is a sliding sign that can be moved to a position that says "Do not Disturb." This sign is for the benefit of anyone who wants to disturb the meeting, including Frank's boss. In the case of his boss, he needs to bring her to this sign and have a discussion with her about it, stressing the importance of not disturbing the meeting. Then, he can invite her to the meeting about a week after the transition and solicit her input. He needs her buy-off on this approach.

The door to the room shall have an electronic lock. Each member of the team that meets in the room will be given an electronic key. Should they choose to use the room other than at production meeting times, they can use their key to obtain access. The computer tied to the key entry will also note the time of entry and exist, hence, if the room is trashed in any way, the culprit can be pinpointed.

Now, the stage is set.

All sorts of enhancements can be added later with the leader's permission as long as they do not clutter the minds of the participants. For instance, an appropriate large digital screen (television) can be used to show production data, graphs or photographs of product or production output of value and interest to the whole group. I just don't recommend starting here even though I mentioned it earlier; let the environment evolve slowly and deliberately.

Never let dazzling "gee-whiz" accessories detract from the meeting's function.

Chapter 4—The Semi or Fully Electronic Meeting

Some project teams have meetings that are all long distance, they never meet together. Others have team members or consultants that are occasionally in the meeting but often participate via an electronic means.

It is important to keep the folks at the end of a wire or fiber optic cable fully engaged.

Be crisp about the way you open the meeting with electronic participants. Everyone should be assigned a number from 1 to "n." The meeting leader opens the meeting by saying "1" (and getting a response of "here"), "2" and so forth. Everyone has a pre-issued dance card with the names, titles, phone numbers and email addresses of the whole team by their assigned number.

If a portion of the group is physically meeting together in a room as we have described previously, they are also assigned a number and are on the dance card. They check in the same way so that the people on the electronic connection know they are there, too.

If the meeting is to start at 09:00 say, all participants need to know they need to be in their places and call in by 08:57. They don't start dialing the phone at 09:00—that is when the meeting starts. Be on time.

Remote participants need to follow the same rules about phones, pagers and so forth plus one more—stay off the computer keyboard during the call. These are close to the microphones and make a tremendous amount of distracting noise in electronic meetings.

It is more important than ever to stick to the agenda with electronic participants.

At the end of the meeting, the leader needs to go around the participants, starting with "1" again and have every participant briefly describe what they are going to be doing in the Coming Period. This way all know that all are working towards the agreed to common goals.

Chapter 5—What is the agenda—(production meeting)?

Once we set the agenda and its order, we can determine who the participants might be. This will be the typical agenda for most production scenarios:

1. Safety Report
2. Excursions from the norm (fire, weather, utility disruptions and so forth)
3. Environmental Report
4. Production volume, other key metrics related to production (water, electricity, and fuel usage for instance)
5. Raw material consumption and costs
6. Quality report
7. Returns and Allowances
8. Production schedule for the next three days
9. Shipping status, inbound and outbound (particularly critical in the colder climates in the winter)
10. Maintenance plans for the next 24 hours and their potential impact on production
11. Chronic maintenance issues and the estimated date each will be solved
12. Capital project status (I would say do this once per week, but it can be missed if it is not in every meeting—start with every meeting and strive to move to once per week after the meeting evolves and you think the agenda is under control)

Then dismiss all that are non-essential and wrap up with

    13. Personnel issues
    14. Hiring status report
    15. Legal issues

This is the standard agenda; there is another agenda needed for a special meeting, but we are not ready for that yet. Stay tuned.

I would give it a few weeks to see if this agenda works in your facility. If it does (or if you modify it), I would then have it printed on high quality stock, framed, and mounted on the wall on one side of the writing surfaces.

Chapter 6—What is the agenda—(project meeting)?

This will be a bit different than the production meeting agenda. It will look more like this:

1. Safety Report
2. Excursions from the norm (fire, weather, utility disruptions and so forth)
3. Environmental Report
4. Milestone progress review
5. Sub milestones reported by each attendee
6. Plans for Coming Period
7. Any anticipated difficulties in meeting plans for Coming Period
8. Any help needed by anyone in Coming Period
9. Agreement on Objectives to be achieved in Coming Period (by each individual in attendance)

Then dismiss all that are non-essential and wrap up with

10. Personnel issues
11. Hiring status report (if necessary)
12. Legal issues

Just like I stated for the production meeting, I would give it a few weeks to see if this agenda works in your facility. If it does (or if you modify it), I would then have it printed on high quality stock, framed and mounted on the wall on one side of the writing surfaces.

Chapter 7—Who attends (production meeting)?

The caustic short answer is—whoever is identified as the manager of each of the points made in Chapter 4. In some cases, personnel may serve double duty. In other cases, the meeting leader may be, for instance, the production manager or hold some other responsibility.

Let's just go through them again to make sure we have the right people in attendance:

1. Safety Report
   a. Safety Manager
   b. The direct supervisor of anyone who was hurt (a special one-time guest to this meeting who will be dismissed after the incident is discussed)
2. Excursions from the norm (fire, weather, utility disruptions and so forth)
   a. Safety Manager
   b. Environmental Manager
3. Environmental Report
   a. Environmental Manager
4. Production volume, other key metrics related to production (water, electrical, and fuel usage for instance)
   a. Production Manager
   b. Utilities Manager
5. Raw material consumption and costs
   a. Raw Material Purchaser

6. Quality report
    a. Technical Department Manager
    b. Tech sales if necessary
7. Returns and Allowances
    a. Sales Manager
    b. Tech sales
8. Production schedule for the next three days
    a. Production Manager
    b. Scheduler
9. Shipping status, inbound and outbound (particularly critical in the colder climates in the winter)
    a. Traffic Manager
10. Maintenance plans for the next 24 hours and their potential impact on production
    a. Maintenance Manger
11. Chronic maintenance issues and the estimated date each will be solved
    a. Maintenance Manager
    b. Engineering Manager
12. Capital project status (I would say do this once per week, but it can be missed if it is not in every meeting—start with every meeting and strive to move to once per week after the meeting evolves and you think it is under control)
    a. Engineering Manager
13. Personnel issues
    a. HR Manager
    b. Legal if local
14. Hiring status report
    a. HR Manager
    b. Manager of Department hiring

15. Legal issues

    a.   Legal if local

Each one of these people, including the overall production meeting leader, has a backup. It is the responsibility of the regular attendees to train their backups, show them the room where the meeting occurs and bring them to the same level of competence at which they are expected to be themselves.

I recommend the backup attend with their manager at least once per quarter, so they can have discussions together about what they mutually saw, the tone and character of the meeting and so forth.

Chapter 8—Who attends (project meeting)?

The caustic short answer is—whoever is identified as the manager of each of the points made in Chapter 5. In some cases, personnel may serve double duty. In most cases the meeting leader will be the project manager or their well-prepared stand-in.

Let's just go through them again to make sure we have the right people in attendance:

1. Safety Report
    a. Safety Manager
    b. The direct supervisor of anyone who was hurt (a special one-time guest to his meeting who will be dismissed after the incident is discussed)
2. Excursions from the norm (fire, weather, utility disruptions and so forth)
    a. Safety Manager
    b. Environmental Manager
3. Environmental Report
    a. Environmental Manager
4. Milestone Progress Review
    a. Each Milestone Leader
    b. Subordinate Managers if appropriate (test for "if appropriate"—can they add value to the meeting?)
5. Sub milestones reported by each attendee

     a. Likely, No. 4 above will have already covered the attendees for this round of reporting

6. Plans for coming period
     a. Each milestone leader (or whomever will be held accountable for each milestone individually)

7. Any anticipated difficulties in meeting plans for Coming Period
     a. Same as above

8. Any help needed by anyone in the Coming Period
     a. Anticipate and bring anyone to the meeting to start with that might be needed here—each milestone leader is responsible for this

9. Agreement on Objectives to be achieved in Coming Period (round robin with eye contact with each individual in the room)

10. Personnel issues
     a. HR Manager
     b. Legal if local

11. Hiring status report
     a. HR Manager
     b. Manager of Department hiring

12. Legal issues
     a. Legal if local

Each one of these people, including the overall project meeting leader, has a backup. It is the responsibility of the regular attendees to train their backups, show them the room where the meeting occurs and bring them to the same level of competence at which they are expected to be themselves.

I recommend the backup attend with their manager at least once per week, so they can have discussions together about what they mutually saw, the tone and character of the meeting and so forth.

Chapter 9—How do the attendees prepare each day?

They conduct their own morning meeting before the facility-wide one. Attendees are trained by their manager to supply the information the Manager needs in order to report to the facility-wide meeting.

Besides the items directly affecting their department, they need to be current on:

1. Safety Report
2. Excursions from the norm (fire, weather, utility disruptions and so forth)
3. Environmental Report

if their department is affected or caused any of these excursions. Others (see Chapters 6 and 7) may report in the facility-wide meeting, but if their department is responsible for any of these, they need to be able to crisply and intelligently contribute to the reporting requirements.

So, I recommend these managers arrive no later than 07:00 for a tour of their area of responsibility. They can have their own department meeting at 08:00 and then be ready for the Facility-wide meeting at 09:00.

These managers will fail if they come to the facility-wide meeting merely regurgitating what they were told earlier by their direct reports. They are expected to prepare their own commentary in compliance with the facility-wide meeting.

The leader may need to offer some private criticism or public praise (see Chapter 11) for the quality of preparation various participants bring to the meeting. The most important thing is to maintain high standards. High standards will be maintained when the leader makes them stick, collectively and individually.

Chapter 10—Report and Pace

The reports and the pace of the meeting are important.

When it comes to reporting, those reporting need to accept responsibility for what they are reporting. If something outside their area of responsibility caused an excursion from the norm, they need to report on it crisply and cleanly, and if the causation manager is in the room, allow that person to remark further.

One bad habit I have seen is that when managers cannot report positively on the performance of their area, they deflect to something else in order to attempt to bring a positive report. One mill where I was witness to this had a twisted way of reporting production. They would report orders for specific customers by grade and tonnage. Since they did not have enough orders to fill their pathetic production schedule, they would continue to make production for inventory of grades they guessed customers would order. Ironically, they called these tons for inventory "On Order" tons when, in reality, they were anything but that.

A new production manager saw right through this and immediately changed the protocol. Hence forth, they reported only the production made for real customers, no matter how many "On Order" tons they had made. He didn't want to hear about them if they were not good tons made for real live, in the present customers. This allowed the responsible production managers to focus on making quality tons for the real customer base and put the sales department on notice that they were not doing their job.

Another matter that is important is to never let anyone volunteer that completing a certain future task is going to be the responsibility of a group of people. There is no such thing as "group accountability"—all accountability is individually based. You likely learned this lesson already if you were ever involved in a group project in school. An individual manager may have a group of individuals to which they parcel out a set of tasks to be completed, hold each of these individuals accountable for their own respective tasks, but group accountability simply doesn't work.

The pace of the meeting is very important and is the responsibility of the leader. Each agenda item and issue brought before the meeting needs to be handled in the correct amount of time for it. Don't watch the clock and think you have to get the meeting done in a certain length of time (although we will expect, with practice, you can hold it to an hour). Also, don't drill into items that are unimportant or should be handled by participants at another time in the Coming Period.

Keep everyone engaged throughout the meeting.

Chapter 11—Preparing for the transition

In order to prepare for the new production meeting format and agenda, the production manager, in this case the hapless Frank, trains each one of his direct reports. While he continues going to and conducting his old-style morning meeting, he also goes to his managers' 08:00 meetings. Sometime, again, one-on-one, he takes them to the new conference room, has them sit where he wants them to sit, and goes through the entire agenda, with timing marks.

He does this one at a time so that he can give each attendee his full attention. He listens to their questions, answers them where he can, and tweaks matters as necessary.

With everything else normally going on, this indoctrination process will take a couple of weeks. That is OK—we want a big buildup to the inaugural day. Let people get their snickers out of their systems, let those defending the new system have a chance to discuss it with the skeptics and thereby help Frank.

Go slowly and develop a big buildup to the new meeting location and style. *You want this to be a big deal—don't rush it.* Spend a lot of time talking to your direct reports about it before you make the change. You may just decide to make some adjustments to your plan before your ever start once you receive this feedback. However, be careful, for if your direct reports see the new level of accountability that is coming, it is likely their suggestions for "improvement" will have a lot to do with not holding them accountable.

After all, if they have been getting by not being accountable until now, they will not want to suddenly take on responsibility—what is in it for them?

So, talk to them frequently, make the new standards clear to them and make sure they understand this will be an uncompromising shift in performance to a higher level.

You may have some participants checking to see if they can retire early or on the phone looking for a new job. That is fine—they are not going to fit in anyway and if they decide on their own to not participate that makes your job easier in the future—you won't have to go through the process of terminating them or have them show up on your unemployment insurance costs.

This is why you should always maintain a professional relationship with all your subordinates. When this relationship becomes too much like a personal friendship, it is difficult, even when necessary, to make the changes the business demands.

Chapter 12—Praise in public, criticize in private

This is basic and you did not have to read this book to know it.

Praise in public, criticize in private.

But why?

So that your direct reports will be sure and always bring you the whole story (this works with your children, too). If you criticize in public, people will quickly start filtering what they tell you and you will not have the full story. Likewise, make sure they understand that this principle travels all the way up and down the reporting chain. You don't want them taking advantage of your policy, then find out they are browbeating their own subordinates.

How do you check up on them? Listen hard to what they say. Watch the mannerisms of their subordinates when you are around them with their bosses present. Do they act differently in front of you when their boss is present than they do when it is one on one? Have your HR Department supply policy training on this subject every six months. The bad actors will be found out shortly—they cannot hide their behavior.

While I say praise in public, do not do this too often, it loses its value. Also keep your own private list of who you have praised so you can randomly rotate the praise around. Think this is silly? One way or another every one of your subordinates is already doing this and comparing the praise they receive to the praise their peers receive. If they have been criticized in pubic, you can be sure they have this etched in stone and know exactly what they have been criticized for doing and have their own opinions as to whether their peers have been criticized for similar missteps.

But to repeat, and more importantly, they will hide anything that fits the pattern in their mind of something that could cause public criticism. This can become very serious. In the safety arena, especially, it can lead to serious accidents, even fatalities.

Chapter 13—Dealing with the non-conformist

You are likely to have one or two people who resist the changes we are talking about in this book. They must be dealt with, or discipline will be lost and the meeting will revert to its old ways thus losing its new-found effectiveness.

Resisters will show up late, show up unprepared, be sullen, or in any number of other ways attempt to be disruptive in a passive-aggressive manner. Start by dealing with them privately—do they understand what is expected of them? Are they untrained in their own role? As leader, your job is to make sure you have given them all the resources possible and they have had a chance to show they know what to do.

If, after your best efforts, they don't come around, it is time for action. How long do you wait to take this action? No more than a month. What is the action? Well, they clearly can't be on the leadership team any longer. They will probably need to leave the company.

I have seen a maintenance manager fired for not bringing a pad of paper and a pencil to the morning meeting (after three warnings). Sends a message.

You want to strike a balance between being compliant and being creative. You do this by setting broad goals in general. Have a problem area? Zero in on it and check the details until you are satisfied it is under control, then back off to a maintenance level when you start seeing stable (and high standards) reporting on the subject.

The motivation of the non-conformist can have many root causes. Maybe they are bored. They may be defiant. You may have taken them outside their comfort zone. If you are going to attempt to save them, you will need to determine their motivations and address those directly.

Chapter 14—Keeping it interesting for the long haul

You may think, having studied this simple book and adopted everything I have said, that your troubles are over. Not hardly!

Routine begets boredom and boredom begets complacency. You are going to have to change it up a bit now and then in order to keep everyone engaged.

Look at long running game shows— "Wheel of Fortune" and "Jeopardy" come to mind. These have been on television for decades, yet their audiences, which attend these airings voluntarily, come back day after day, week after week, year after year.

If you watch carefully, these shows do not change the basic premise, nor the music, or even the hosts (just how old are Pat Sajak, Vanna White and Alex Trebek?). What they do do, however, is make small and subtle tweaks to the way the game is played, the rewards, other minor items. Their objective is to keep it familiar but interesting.

One great production meeting leader I watched would occasionally, at the beginning of the meeting, ask the participants a question to which he thought they all should know the answer. He would pass out slips of paper, ask them to provide the answer and sign their names. He gave a spot award ($50 gift certificate) to those who answered correctly. He was not mechanical about this—sometimes it would happen about six weeks apart, other times two weeks, other times three months. And the questions were all over the map—but each were about things he thought each participant should know.

Another great leader I have known particularly liked to take field trips with the production meeting team after the meeting on Saturday and Sunday mornings. He didn't do it every week, but he did it often. They would file out to see a certain problem, then file back to the production meeting room to brainstorm solutions. It is amazing how fast people can come up with good solutions to seemingly intractable problems on Saturday or Sunday mornings!

Sometimes it is good to physically turn the room around. People become used to sitting in the same places, saying the same things.

You can alter the sequence of reports (as long as you keep safety as #1—it never moves in the agenda).

I have seen managers take an extra half hour, on Fridays, for instance, to have an individual department make a presentation to the whole group about how they are organized, the details of their mission and so forth. This can initiate real, constructive change in the way the business is operated. It will certainly inform everyone else about the mysterious workings of departments they have spent little time focusing on in the past.

Chapter 15—The Most Important Meeting

You thought the production or project meeting occurring each morning was the most important meeting? I have led you astray...the most important meeting is at 2:30 or 3:00 pm on Friday afternoon (depends on when your normal quitting time is).

This is the weekend preparation meeting. It is vital for every five-day and seven-day operation and is a luxury that project teams should use.

You may protest if you run a five-day operation—after all, your operation is likely shut down over the weekend. Let me ask you this question? Will anything be going on in your operation before your morning production meeting reconvenes on Monday? I thought so.

Some operations start at midnight on Sunday, some with gluing operations require glue pots or other devices to be started three hours before actual production commences. We are now at 9:00 pm Sunday night. What can go wrong? Who should be called if something does go wrong?

Of course, five-day operations often schedule maintenance and major project installations on the weekends. These can be especially worrisome, particularly if contractors are involved. Are all the required components, down to the gaskets, nuts and bolts on site? Is everyone trained in safety and LOTO (Lock Out

Tag Out)? On and on and on—the questions can be quite detailed and specific.

For seven-day operations, the task is actually a bit simpler:

1. Make sure all weak or limping systems have complete coverage and those responsible for weekend duty know what to do if they fail (again, down to the last gasket, nut and bolt).
2. The production runs and grades set for the weekend are the simplest and easiest in your whole schedule.
3. NEVER EVER run trials on the weekend. There is not enough support available if something should go wrong.

In all cases, go over who is on call for the weekend, under what criteria they are to be called, and, for once bring the phones in the room that they will be carrying and dial every last one of them and make sure they are working. I don't care if you did it last Friday with the same people, do it again.

Chapter 16—When it is necessary to operate in extremis

Sometimes conditions have gotten very difficult. Perhaps there was a catastrophe, a major equipment failure, a sudden loss of key personnel.

In these cases, the routine meetings described up to this point are not enough. Your direct reports need to "check out" with you each evening before they go home.

This is beyond them stopping by your office and waving as they run for the parking lot. They come with a report on the key items that were agreed to in the production meeting that day and distinct plans on the progress to be made overnight. Who is in charge? What will they do? What are their trigger points to call for backup and who do they call? How often are they expected to report in overnight?

You get the idea. If you are in extremis, it is all hands on deck until the condition or conditions pass that is/are causing the problem.

Someone "forgot" to check out with you before heading home? Call them up, have them physically come back and report on the critical items under their purview. Don't let them off with a phone call.

Chapter 17—Don't forget the big picture

I started this book talking about you getting a better night's sleep. That is your personal goal. The company's goal is to "spin the invoice printer."

Many people think they can take shortcuts and avoid the subjects covered in this little book, still achieving a good night's sleep, and maximizing the profitability of the assets under their control.

In close to forty-eight years in manufacturing businesses, I have never seen this happen. The shortest path to profitability and a good night's sleep is the path I have outlined in this book.

People do not, at least in a reliable enough fashion to count on, rise up on their own, do the tasks and develop the attitudes described in this book without the proper leadership to create and maintain these institutions.

I referred to sports teams earlier. I stated every sports team has production meetings. These are meetings with distinct features, agendas and proper motivational activities. In some ways, sports teams are more fortunate and have a better chance of achieving their objectives than we do in manufacturing. For one thing, our pace is too slow—a twenty-four-hour cycle (unless you are doing the 24 hours at Le Mans) is leisurely as compared to a sporting event. By the way, do you know 24-hour race car drivers urinate and defecate in their suits? —they know, thoroughly understand, and are committed to the objective at hand. The other great thing about sports teams is this—the players know if they don't perform they will be traded or terminated. We do not deal this harshly with non-performance in manufacturing industries. We give people another chance, we send them to more training and on and on and on.

But I digress—follow the guidance in this book and I am certain you'll make your goals, personally and professionally.

www.ingramcontent.com/pod-product-compliance
Lightning Source LLC
Chambersburg PA
CBHW030932220326
41521CB00039B/2145